Transformational Journaling for Recovering Souls:
15 Guided Techniques to Recreate Your Life

Debra A. Wingfield, Ed.D., LPC

Wingfield House of Peace Publications

Wingfield House of Peace Publications
Pueblo West, CO

Copyright © 2007 Debra A. Wingfield, Ed.D., LPC

All rights reserved
This book is protected by United States of America copyright protections. No part of this publication may be reproduced, stored in a retrieval system or transmitted in any form or by any means, electronic, mechanical, photocopying, recording or otherwise without the written permission of the publisher.

ISBN 978-0-6151-4460-3

How to Contact the Author

Debra A. Wingfield, Ed.D., LPC,
Wingfield House of Peace Publications
Pueblo West, CO
Phone: 719.647.0652
DrDebra@houseofpeacepubs.com
Web site: www.houseofpeacepubs.com

Here's what people are saying about *Transformational Journaling for recovering Souls: 15 Guided Techniques to Recreate Your Life*

Transformational Journaling for Recovering Souls is an easy read...a good tool to learn how to journal. Anyone picking up this short book/journal can address their self-esteem, self-confidence, or trauma issues. I recommend it as an adjunct to therapy, for addiction treatment aftercare, or abuse survivors to maintain recovery.

> Teresa J. Marshall, Ph.D., Clinical Psychologist,
> Director, Parkview Medical Center Chemical Dependency Unit

I enjoyed your book very much.

> Erik Stone, Director of Quality Assurance, Signal Behavioral Health Network, Denver, CO

Acknowledgements

To my loving husband, Charles, to my daughter, Michele, and my stepson, Phillip for all their support through the years.

To my higher power, whom I choose to call God, for showing me the path of healing and compassion for those still in pain, and the ability to pass healing tools onto others.

To my clients, teachers, and friends who have encouraged me along the way.

To my mentors Jeanetta Blazek, Centa Terry, and Janet Henze and all my Klemmer friends for believing in me. To my buddy and mastermind partners who encouraged me to step outside the box and held me accountable through the rough times.

To my readers/editors Muriel Kallick, Pamela Arwine, and Pamela Grills who took time out from their busy lives to read and edit drafts of this book.

Thank you for your love and direction.

Transformational Journaling for Recovering Souls:
15 Guided Techniques to Recreate Your Life

TABLE OF CONTENTS

- PREFACE: AN EXPERIENTIAL APPROACH 8
- TRANSFORMATIONAL JOURNALING 11
    - Transformational Journaling 12
    - The Process of Recovery 13
    - Tools of Recovery 20
    - Journaling/Writing 20
    - Issue Journaling 22
    - Feelings Journaling 22
    - Musings 23
- PATTERN IDENTIFICATION AND REFRAMING 27
    - Family Characteristics 28
    - Family Roles 34
    - Family Rules 38
- FEELINGS CENTERED JOURNALING 44
    - Drawing Faces To Represent Feelings 45
    - Describing Feelings 47
    - Carried Feelings 52
    - Grief and Loss 54
- THOUGHT CENTERED JOURNALING 58
    - Boundary Setting 59
    - Polarized Thinking 64
- MAINTAINING RECOVERY 69
    - Affirmations 70
    - Creating a Balanced Lifestyle 74
    - Sharing with Others 78
- APPENDIX A: 80
    - FEELING WORDS 80

TABLE of TABLES

- Table 1 Family Characteristics 30
- Table 2 Family Rules 41
- Table 3 Describing Feelings 49
- Table 4 Polarized Thinking 67

PREFACE: An Experiential Approach

Transformational Journaling is a process I developed while going through recovery from my second marriage to an untreated alcoholic. During my recovery process, I discovered the impact of childhood incest by my father. This lead to more intensive recovery work including returning to therapy that was finally successful. Previous therapy failed to address the underlying impacts of incest. This made it easy for me to slip into a marriage with an alcoholic. I am blessed with a wonderful husband today (my third) who is a recovering alcoholic. You can read my recovery story in <u>From Darkness to Light: An Incest Survivor's Recovery Journey Through Transformational Journaling</u>. It addresses these events.

The Transformational Journaling techniques described in this book were put together for groups offered to adults from alcoholic, abusive, and other dysfunctional family backgrounds. Over twelve weeks, clients learned about their family-of-origin patterns using these tools. By applying these techniques in their daily lives, they made conscious choices about changes they wanted to create. Now you have an opportunity to apply these techniques in your daily life.

In my experience, the best way to achieve maximum results with these tools is through written journaling. There are many ways to do this including using the journaling exercises throughout this book. If you prefer to use your computer to write your journal, I suggest you put it in a password protected file.

Another alternative is to speak into a tape recorder or other recording device. The disadvantage to this method is you miss seeing what you have put down. You are less likely to go back and listen in the future. By having written words, you have an opportunity to go back and identify patterns. You can learn from them as well as make conscious choices for change.

Some people get stuck on writing because of concerns about spelling, punctuation, and grammar. Set aside your concerns for the above as this journal is for you. If you choose to share it, you will probably do so verbally. In my book <u>From Darkness to Light: An Incest Survivor's Recovery Journey Through Transformational Journaling,</u> you will notice incorrect grammar and punctuation.

Another set of questions I am asked when I recommend journaling are related to how often to journal, when to journal, and how much do I journal? My response is to find a quiet place and time of day when you are least likely to be interrupted. Set aside 10-15 minutes daily as you learn these techniques. You may choose to journal for a longer period of time. However, establishing a set time and location is the process for building your journaling habit. Reflect on your day and find what works best for you.

When I first started journaling, I found the first 10-15 minutes when I went to bed worked best for me. This is my relaxing and unwinding time to read before going to sleep. Adding journaling for the first 10 minutes gives me time to reflect on my day. Find what works best for you and establish a daily journaling pattern. So, relax, enjoy the process, and let your words flow.

> Throughout this book, there are starter exercises to give you a taste of journaling. You may find you have more to write than the space available. There are additional journaling pages at the back of the book where you can continue your journaling process.

The exercises found throughout the book are based on those used in groups offered for my clients. Each exercise is identified in italics with an example. Then, you are provided an opportunity to respond to the exercise. You may choose to read through the entire book, then return to do the exercises. I recommend you do each exercise as you come to it to reinforce your understanding of how the exercise works for you.

Please feel free to contact me with questions about the exercises at questions@houseofpeacepubs.com.

Disclaimer: This book is a method of journaling. It is not intended to take the place of therapy.

SECTION I

TRANSFORMATIONAL JOURNALING

Transformational journaling is a process of internal inquiry about life events and the impacts they have on your functioning. Through *Transformational journaling*, you have an opportunity to explore thinking and behavior patterns and the underlying feelings attached to them. You, then, determine if they are conscious choices or ingrained from childhood experiences. Once these thinking and behavior patterns are revealed, you have an opportunity to choose to continue with those patterns or to make conscious changes if those patterns are no longer serving you.

There are a number of techniques offered in this book that you may find useful at different times in the journey of recovering your soul. There is no set order in which to go through various techniques. By reviewing and understanding the purpose of each technique, you are able to select what is most meaningful to you as you proceed through the recovery process. You may find you use more than one technique in a journaling session depending on what patterns you identify and how you want to work with those patterns.

Explore and work with each technique to find out what helps in your recovery. This journal is not designed to take the place of working with a therapist. However, you may find this journal helpful in your therapeutic process.

My wish for you is you will find these techniques helpful in your recovery. Many of my therapy clients were able to move more quickly through their recovery using these techniques. One woman, who experienced emotional sexual abuse, found she could quickly discover what triggered her emotional over-reaction by quieting her mind and focusing on her pain through writing about how the trigger related to her childhood. May you find the same emotional and mental release from the events in your life as the individuals I was privileged to walk with in their recovery.

You may choose to start or end each journaling session with a list of three to five things you are grateful for in your life on that particular day. Gratitude helps maintain balance while you are exploring the impacts of your life. Being able to notice a flower blooming, a beautiful sunset, or a special moment with a family member is an important part of healing.

THE PROCESS OF RECOVERY

This is a lifetime process of discovering who you are. The process occurs on a continuum. You can be at many points on the continuum depending on the thoughts and feelings you are experiencing at any given time. As recovery progresses, you will spend more time at the self-love end of the continuum than at the denial end. The process of recovery goes through the stages on this continuum.

| DENIAL | AWARENESS | HEALING | COMPASSION AND ACCOUNTABILITY | SELF-LOVE |

Briefly defined, the five stages are:

Denial--being in your survival pattern.

Awareness--getting in touch with feeling memories. Thinking about how you feel versus experiencing your feelings.

Healing--identification, determining who you are; what you stand for; reestablishing the ability to think, feel and act for yourself by finding your inner child of the past; developing motivation for maintaining your autonomy.

Compassion and Accountability--understanding your family history and being able to let go of the past to forgive yourself and others; being responsible for your actions and holding others accountable for theirs.

Self-love--being able to love yourself and accept yourself unconditionally wherever you are in the process.

Let's review the process of recovery in more detail. When you are in d*enial*, you are in your survival pattern. Whatever role you learned as a child, you use in your daily life and relationships. These refer to the roles of: mascot, caretaker, scapegoat, lost child and hero. You discover the role most productive for you. Roles permitted you to get strokes and recognition and helped maintain the family balance. Many people stay in denial about their lives forever.

If you choose recovery, you may find a willingness to come out of denial in some areas of your life. However, you may fear facing other areas and continue to struggle with a level of pain.

A willingness to look at all areas of your life may take the rest of your life. This requires a willingness to walk through all the pain and move to the other side.

Once you commit yourself to this path, the positive route is lifelong learning and personal development. The negative route is mental illness, insanity, and for some, return to destructive patterns or addictions. Is it worth it? You must decide for yourself. For many, it is worth it. Once you are on the other side of the pain, the freedom you experience makes it worth going through the pain.

How do you break through your *denial?* It comes a piece at a time as you are willing to be aware of pain in different areas of your life. The pain comes from past events triggering old feelings as you are experiencing seemingly new situations. In reality, many of these new situations are just replays of old tapes with new players and new surroundings.

Only when you get to the root of the script are you able to rewrite it. In soul recovery, this is called getting your history straight. To figure out your history, you need to be willing to move past denial into awareness.

In *awareness*, your eyes are opened to your feelings, behaviors, and thought patterns. You know there is a sense of discomfort and a desire to stop being in pain. Moving into awareness, you experience many different levels of understanding about your history.

First, you begin to understand from an intellectual or thought-based standpoint. You read self-help books, listen to how others have understood their lives, and use logic and thinking to explain your process. Then, you become aware of your feelings about that piece of history. However, at this point, actually feeling your feelings inside your body may be too overwhelming. This is a process. You do it at the rate you can handle. The information and feelings need to be addressed at your pace.

The process may uncover a surface feeling triggered by a situation currently happening in your life. As you explore the feeling, you may find it is stronger and more intense. By continuing to focus on the feeling triggered with the event, you come to the root feeling tied to the childhood event. This opens the memory of the original event.

After you acknowledge your memory of the experience and identify your feelings, move into experiencing these feelings in your body. You were probably cut off from your feelings for a long time. Therefore, it may take a long time to recover the feelings related to the experience.

You may talk about the incident and acknowledge the feelings without actually showing the depth of the feeling. Then you accept your feelings and the fact they are healthy and valid for the situation. Finally, you give yourself permission to experience the feelings on a bodily level.

Once you allow yourself to experience the feelings, you move to the next area of the continuum--*healing*. In the *healing* process, you begin to form your identity around the issue, determining your own beliefs and values about your past history. At this point, you begin to allow your whole self to emerge and respond to what you learned. You reconnect with the inner child of the past and allow the Child's response to the feelings to reoccur and come out. As you integrate all parts of the personality to relive and experience the issue, a sense of completeness and serenity surrounds you. This is another level of acceptance.

As you heal from the experience, you develop the ability to have *compassion* coupled with holding yourself and others *accountable* for the impact on your past. You are able to let go of the pain and experience the comfort of peace and serenity. This process, many times, is a stumbling block as you may tend to continue to use the old family messages about what you are supposed to be, have, and do.

These messages or patterns tend to keep you bouncing back and forth from wanting to be *compassionate* to yourself and wanting to punish yourself for your past. This can keep you locked into feeling worthless and inadequate and promotes a fear response. These old rules gave you a sense of existence and if you let go of them, you fear your greatest fear, that you will indeed be invisible.

Accountability is a subset of *compassion*. It is being responsible for your actions and holding others responsible for their actions. Your compassion and understanding about how others learned their behavior patterns allows you to release your anger toward them and creates forgiveness. At the same time, every person is *accountable* for the choices they make and the impact of their actions on others.

Holding yourself *accountable* means doing the work of recovery and healing. Holding others *accountable* means they are responsible for doing whatever it takes to be responsible toward those they harmed and to heal and come to terms with what happened in their lives.

Finally, *self-love* emerges. You begin to accept yourself unconditionally and stand in life as you truly are, unmasked and available as a whole human being. You remain at this end of the continuum as long as you are not experiencing pain. *Self-love* allows freedom of expression of who you are, what you stand for, and establishes healthy, loving boundaries with others in all interactions.

What happens when another trigger comes along and calls to mind an incident out of the past? You move back along the continuum to work through the process again. You may initially go into *denial* or choose to stop at *awareness* and work through the process from there. As you gain in your recovery, the time you spend working through each part of the continuum is lessened if you allow yourself to be in the process instead of fighting it.

It is only when you rebel against experiencing the process that the pain becomes more intense. Eventually, you choose either the positive route of moving through the process on this new issue or the negative path of insanity, return to self-destructive patterns, or death. For recovering souls, many times the only options they can see are suicide or insanity. The thought of walking through another painful issue seems too overwhelming. J was sure his wife would not return to him and his children were closely tied to her. He was ready to give up. Then he decided his life was worth fighting for and he wanted his wife and children back. Through his recovery process in therapy and involvement in Narcotics Anonymous, he found answers leading to reconciliation with his family.

This is one reason I strongly recommend all people in recovery become involved with some type of support system that fosters their recovery process. In addition to support groups, individual and group therapy can enable a recovering soul to work through their own recovery process and focus on individual issues. Any other forms of stimuli that assist the recovering soul in moving out of denial and into recovery are strongly recommended.

TOOLS OF RECOVERY

What are the specific tools to guide a person through recovery? These take many different forms. What I found most useful is a combination of techniques covered in this journal. I provide exercises throughout this book to apply in your own recovery process.

JOURNALING/WRITING

There are many methods for journaling that are designed to help people get in touch with their feelings and to work through their issues. One technique I find works best when getting started is to begin where you are and write about how you are feeling at the moment, what has happened in your day or whatever comes out of your pen at the moment. This is called *stream-of-consciousness writing*.

This helps people get in touch with who they are. It is a good way to begin your recovery as many recovering souls find it difficult to write anything about their personal thoughts and self-understanding. This often comes from being out of touch with you.

Plan to write daily for ten to fifteen minutes in the beginning just to become acquainted with your life as you are presently living it.

Write about what happened in your day _____
_____
_____
_____

Who did you encounter? _____
_____
_____

Were there any significant issues that you were able to identify? _____
_____
_____
_____

Think out loud on paper, on your computer, or audio record whatever flows through your mind. Right now you are building your journaling muscle and giving yourself permission to move thoughts out of your head and onto paper, typed in your computer or audio recording, to become acquainted with your self-talk.

Start right now by identifying an incident from your day and letting your thoughts flow.

My incident today was _____
_____
_____

My thoughts about it are _____

_____

_____

ISSUE JOURNALING

The next step I recommend in journaling is writing when an issue comes up. Allow the pen to go as the thoughts come to you. This helps to clarify the issue and get it out of your head. Then, you can see it and have a greater sense of the reality of the issue. You may come up with some surprising information you were subconsciously keeping out of your awareness by keeping all this in your head.

The issue that came up for me was _____

_____

_____

What I think about that is _____

_____

_____

FEELINGS JOURNALING

Write about a feeling that was triggered for you. Write the answer to this question I learned from Pia Mellody (1986) from her audio tapes "Permission to be Precious".

> *Where in my history have I felt this way before or experienced a similar incident before?* _____
>
> _____
>
> _____
>
> _____

Write about a feeling you experienced recently and go back in your history to find the root. Going backwards in time is the best way to get connected with this information. If you find you are blocked at some point, make up what you think happened and be very clear this is what you are doing. If you find the experience remains the same over the next 24-48 hours, then you can be relatively sure this is what happened. If you suddenly have a different memory, then you need to write it down and refer back to what you made up and see it as a trigger to where you were hiding information from your conscious mind.

MUSINGS

Write on a specific topic or issue you want to address. This helps you understand your thoughts about it. This helps to separate your beliefs and thoughts from parents and primary caregivers. I call this *"musings"*. You may surprise yourself at the depth of your thinking. It is possible you will gain some intuitive insights just below your level of awareness. Allow the pen to put down whatever comes to your mind without judging or censoring your thoughts.

For example, on one occasion I wrote about how I wanted to parent my teenage daughter. This is from my book <u>From Darkness to Light: An Incest Survivor's Recovery Journey through Transformational Journaling</u>.

> *"What do I consider as a parent reasonable, responsible behavior from Michele? Based on her abilities, I consider it reasonable to ask that her clothes be taken care of properly. By that I mean, clean clothes put away in drawers or hung up and dirty clothes placed in her hamper. I expect Michele to keep her room in reasonably neat order, dusted and vacuumed every two to three weeks and all dishes and glasses put in the dishwasher daily. I feel Michele is responsible for seeing this gets done without having to be reminded each time it needs doing.*
>
> *I consider it reasonable for Michele to keep her bathroom neat -- towels hung on racks and countertop orderly with things put away daily. I feel Michele's bathroom needs to be cleaned every two weeks. That means cleaning sink and counter, toilet and bathtub with proper cleaners. The floor needs washing monthly.*

Michele has accepted the responsibility for washing her own clothes and she may choose to wash hers when I wash mine or separately. I let her know when I am washing so she can get her clothes to the basement or not as she chooses.

As to keeping the house clean and picked up, I have listed all the items that need to be done. I've agreed with Michele to put them up in full view and to ask her to do one or two daily Monday through Friday. I write Michele notes daily as to what is to be done and the agreement is that it will be done by 5:00 p.m. otherwise she will not be allowed to go out. These are rotated as much as possible. With school starting, the responsibility for Michele completing her homework rests with her. I want to be shown the completed product daily and will not correct or request changes be made. I expect neat, legible work that shows thought and effort on her part. I request weekly grades in order for Michele to go out on weekends.

I expect to be told the truth and if I am lied to the consequences will be tied directly to the issue as has been my discipline procedure since Michele was a small child.

Michele is responsible for keeping herself neat, clean and presentable and for appearing that way before any friends, male or female who come to our home.

I expect Michele to have the same pride in herself and her home as she sees demonstrated by me. Michele has three pets which she has asked for and indicated she would be responsible for. In order to keep her pets, she is responsible for feeding them and grooming them and caring for their waste products. This should be done with little or preferably no prompting from me."

What is a pressing issue in your life today?

_____
_____
_____
_____
_____

To summarize, being flexible with these techniques allows you to choose what you feel gets you to the base of the issue. Sometimes you lose touch with where you are and you just need to get connected again. Sometimes you have feelings triggered and issue writing is most helpful. At other times you may feel you have a specific topic or issue that you understand at some level and want to know just how far along the continuum you are with it. These journaling tools are helpful in various situations.

SECTION II
PATTERN IDENTIFICATION AND REFRAMING

In addition to the less structured journaling techniques, I found it helpful for individuals to describe patterns based on various *specific areas identified in family dynamics*. Family dynamics are the interactional processes and behaviors of family members within the family system (Olson, McCubbin & Associates, 1983). In other words, how family members relate to each other. These include family characteristics, family roles, and family rules.

FAMILY CHARACTERISTICS

Healthy family characteristics are important in creating a healthy functioning family. The more a family functions on a healthy level day-by-day, the more quickly they return to healthy functioning after moving through a crisis or stress situation. Fogarty (1976), and Goldenberg and Goldenberg (1980) define functional family characteristics. They separate them into four areas: relationships, communication, personal growth, and system maintenance. These are described in Table 1.

Let's take an example of how to work with Family Characteristics (Table 1). Using the first characteristic related to stress and strain, I would rate my family of origin as a 3. In my family when stress occurred outside our daily functioning, my mother and father would immediately move in to tell the person experiencing stress how to fix it. They believed their answers were the only right answers and would not listen to feelings, concerns, or other ideas. Their goal was to get everything back into their control. Family members who encountered stress were left to work through their emotional pain alone.

Follow the instructions for rating your family on each characteristic. Then describe the patterns as you saw them expressed.

Rate your family characteristics from 5-1 as applies to your family of origin with 5 being functional and 1 being dysfunctional. (Many people like to view current family as well.) Put an "O" by each characteristic for family of origin, then redoing the characteristics with "C" for current family. Then, go through each of the four areas and identify one pattern that you can describe from your family system as an example of how your family operated.

For additional benefit, review each characteristic, rate it, then write out how your family-of-origin operated based on your description. The best method to see this is through examples of what occurred in your family. Finally, you can determine what you would like to do differently in the future. This provides an opportunity for you to restructure the behavior and thinking around that particular characteristic.

Table 1 Family Characteristics

(Rate your family of origin on a scale from 5-1 with five being functional and one being dysfunctional.)

	FUNCTIONAL COMMUNICATION	DYSFUNCTIONAL
	Each family member is able to cope with stress and strain and support members to recover quickly.	There may be a temporary breakdown in ability to deal with stress and strain. No individual support available to other family members.
	Family members communicate thoughts and feelings openly and honestly in all areas.	Communications are often guarded or painful when necessary, may be distant or hostile.
	Communications with one another are caring, open, understanding, and trusting.	Parents team up against children creating power struggles.
	Family members show respect for one's own views and those of others.	Family members feel hindered in expressing their own views and opinions.
	Each person feels free to be honest about thoughts and feelings in agreeing or disagreeing.	One member dominates and insists others submit.

	Parents and children have opinions, negotiations are common.	Members apt to feel alone and to respond to one another in a helpless, powerless or controlled fashion.
	Each twosome can deal with all problems that occur between them. Problems are handled directly.	Message carrying often occurs to solve problems by going through one person to talk to another.
	FUNCTIONAL RELATIONSHIPS	**DYSFUNCTIONAL**
	There is respect for autonomy—toleration of individuality and separateness.	Members expected to be either close together or to be totally apart or to bounce in between.
	Family members can adapt to and even welcome change.	Rigidity is rewarded and change is discouraged.
	Emotional problems are seen as existing in the family unit, with pieces in each person.	Emotional problems are seen within one person and not a problem of any other members.
	Family members maintain contact across generations.	Generations may be totally alienated from one another.
	FUNCTIONAL PERSONAL GROWTH	**DYSFUNCTIONAL**
	Each person understands how to get what he needs from himself and from others.	Everyone is busy seeing to others' needs to the exclusion of their own.
	Each person is allowed to have his/her own feelings and they are accepted as valid.	Feelings expressed may be invalidated if considered unacceptable for the situation.

	Each person is allowed times of dependence, independence, and interdependence as appropriate.	Members are expected to be too dependent or must totally rely on themselves. There is no allowance for interdependence.
	The protection of a "positive" emotional climate takes priority over what "should" be done and what is "right".	Rules of the family are more important than the individual.
	FUNCTIONAL SYSTEM MAINTENANCE	**DYSFUNCTIONAL**
	Parents establish the functioning of the total family by meeting wants and needs of themselves and children.	Parents look to children to fill their wants and needs.
	Parents offer family leadership as well as model relating to others.	Parents go from one extreme to the other trying to be adults, then acting like children— they lack sense of who they are.
	Family members actively do things together and each member can come up with ideas for activities.	Family members avoid being together in activities.
	Power resides in the parental team.	Children often have more power than parents.

	Health in the family is determined by each member saying this is a pretty good family to live in over time. If one or more members say there is a problem, there is a problem and it is addressed.	Members want to separate as soon as possible or are too dependent to leave at all. No one can point out a problem or problems are ignored.
	Members in the family can use others in the family as a source of information about how others view them to change unhealthy behaviors.	Members in the family are viewed as the enemy. They refuse or deny information about themselves to change unhealthy behaviors.

Describe what your family did related to the characteristic identified
_____
_____
_____
_____

How do you want to do this differently in the future? _____
_____
_____
_____
_____

Use this technique for as many characteristics as you want to change. I encourage you to come back to this table and review your progress or write about other characteristics as you discover them.

FAMILY ROLES

In functional families, emotional responsibilities are fluid, moving from family member to family member as the need arises. In dysfunctional families, these roles tend to be assigned and remain rigidly entrenched. As the child moves into an adult relationship, they take their emotional role with them expecting their partner to balance them out with the partner's assigned role from their family-of-origin.

These rigid emotional roles help to identify the expected emotional role of the designated family member. Often these roles are assigned based on birth order with the oldest being given the role of *Hero* or *Caretaker*, the middle child identified as the *Scapegoat*, the third child the *Lost Child*, and the youngest, the *Mascot*.

Review the family role definitions and define what role fits you and how you experience it in your life and relationships today. You may find yourself in one or more roles. The role where you spend most of your time is the one to look at more deeply. This may be how you operate outside your family as well.

For example, it is fairly common to see these roles operating in a work setting where you spend most of your time. How does this affect your work relationships? Are people hired to fill a role more than meeting job requirements? This is just another place to explore this pattern.

Hero--person who sees and hears what is happening and takes responsibility for the family by becoming successful and popular. The emotional role for this person is to make the family look good to the outside world. They appear to have it all together and look good publicly. These are often the presidents or CEOs of companies, or people with highly successful careers. They experience internal pressure from the family to have the **right** home, the **right** family, the **right** career, and to lead the family through crises and chaotic situations. These are the **"look good"** family members.

Emotionally, these children and adults suffer from lack of personal identity. They are the family identity. They are uptight, perfectionistic, and always in control on the outside. Internally, they experience a lot of stress that can lead to stress-related physical health problems. They never feel they are good enough. They have a pessimistic view of life, and have difficulty making changes.

Caretaker or enabler--person who does "everything under the sun" to make the dysfunctional or addicted person stop, everything, except what works: confronting the user or leaving the relationship. This role is often combined with the Hero role when there are not enough family members available to carry all the roles.

Emotionally, these children feel overburdened with responsibility for everyone else to the exclusion of their own lives. They are in last place in their own minds. Everyone and everything comes first. They see themselves as nurturing and caregivers to their family, friends, and even strangers. They tend to be optimists and see the good in everyone and everything.

Scapegoat (victim)--rejects the family system by running away, withdrawal, or defiant behavior. The goal for this family member is to take the heat off the person with the real problem and focus all the attention on their acting out behavior. When they become tired of always taking the heat for their behavior, they may completely withdraw from the family system. This can be through cutting off communication, being in jail or just disappearing and creating a life disconnected from the family. However, they still carry the scapegoat (victim) role with them into their relationships and friendships.

Emotionally, they tend to act out the anger they carry from the family in passive-aggressive relationships, or outright uncontrolled anger that leads to criminal behavior.

Lost child--quietly and unobtrusively withdraws from the family system. This child is more a wallflower than a participator. They blend into the woodwork whenever possible. Their role is to avoid making waves or be noticed. They take supportive positions in their relationships and work. When the spotlight focuses on them, they are able to push someone else forward so they can disappear from the situation.

Emotionally, they look very independent while they are crying inside from lack of attention. They tend to brush over any concerns about themselves to keep from being noticed. They are effective at entertaining themselves and passing off any pursuit of involvement as being happy doing things on their own. This person may be the scapegoat in disguise when there are not enough children to pass the roles around in the family.

Mascot-- hides his pain with humor and provides "comic relief" in the family. This is often the cute, funny child who takes the pressure off the family when tensions build too high. This is the practical jokester, the prankster who rarely shows a serious side. Their main focus is creating a distraction from the real problems in the family. Often, this is the youngest child who is not held to the same level of responsibility as older children. They are the cute baby who grows up to be the cute kid that everybody loves.

Emotionally, they want to be held to the same standard as the other children in the family. They want fair and equal treatment instead of special treatment. Often, they end up in the spotlight as adults as comedians who provide entertainment to the family and the world.

> *Describe how you see your role in your family.* _____
>
> _____
>
> _____
>
> _____
>
> _____
>
> *Write out how you want to transform yourself without being stuck in one specific role.* _____
>
> _____
>
> _____
>
> _____

FAMILY RULES

Family rules are expectations about how family members interact or relate to each other. They may be stated or unstated. When family rules are stated, they may or may not use the wording used in Table 2.

In dysfunctional families, family rules keep members from growing and developing emotionally in a healthy way. They stifle the natural spontaneity of the human being. By following the dysfunctional family rules, the individual is set up to become an adult child.

An adult child is an individual who carries the dysfunctional messages, behaviors, and patterns of the family

Pattern Identification and Reframing 39

system into their adult lives and relationships. When emotional or stressful situations arise, they revert back to learned responses from their childhood.

How you respond to family rules defines the direction of your adult child behavior patterns. This does not necessarily dictate the type of behavior you will chose, only the way you will act out your behaviors.

In order to change the dysfunctional rules and stop the adult child behavior, it is necessary to identify how the rules were stated and understood. Then, reword the messages to allow healthy rules to take their place. To accomplish this, ask yourself what are the sub-rules that functioned in your family under each of the nine general rules.

For example, using the first rule, this would be stated in the following way: this family does not have problems. If you have a problem, don't let anyone know. If it really starts to bother you, talk about it passive-aggressively by dropping hints, saying things in passing or on the run so there won't be time to talk about the issue. Just say what it is and don't expect to get a response. If you do get a response, it will be indirectly and you'll have to guess at what the response truly is.

Your family may have a different pattern for this rule. Go ahead and *write out what you experienced*. As you review the rules in Table 2, rate 5-1 as it applies to your family of origin with 5 being healthy and 1 being unhealthy. (Many people like to view current family as well. Put an "O" with the number by each rule for family of origin. Reread the rules using "C" for current family.) These are just a few of the rules. As you look at your family, you will start to see what some of the specific rules are in your family. Then, journal using the following format:

Write out how the rule was expressed and experienced in your family
_____
_____
_____
_____

Write out how you want to transform the rule without being stuck in one expression and experience of the rule _____
_____
_____
_____

Continue to do this with each of the rules in Table 2.

Write out how the rule was expressed and experienced in your family
_____
_____
_____

Write out how you want to transform the rule without being stuck in one expression and experience of the rule _____
_____

Table 2 Family Rules

FUNCTIONAL/HEALTHY	DYSFUNCTIONAL/UNHEALTHY
1) It's OK to talk about problems and to ask for outside help if needed.	1) Talking about problems inside or outside the family is unacceptable.
2) It's OK to talk about and express feelings openly.	2) Talking about or expressing feelings that are unacceptable is forbidden.
3) Direct communication with the person is regarded as necessary to resolve differences.	3) Using someone or something to send your message indirectly (triangulation).
4) Realistic expectations are made of each person as they are seen as imperfect and human.	4) Expectations are unrealistic and expressed through indirect or comparative methods.
5) Each person is self-responsible, caring for their own thoughts, feelings and actions.	5) Taking care of yourself is seen as being selfish.
6) Parents are consistent modeling the behavior they describe as acceptable.	6) Parents are inconsistent, telling children to do as they are told, even when parents do something different.
7) It's OK to play and have fun even when there are other things to do. Taking a break is rejuvenating.	7) Having fun comes after everything else is done and that only happens on rare occasions.
8) It's OK to adjust to change, to face issues and grow through problems to be whole, healthy, autonomous human beings.	8) Change is unacceptable. There is only one way and that is the right way.
9) It's OK to talk about sex and relationships, especially the emotional part.	9) Talking about sex or relationships is forbidden. (Adapted from Subby, 1987)

When you describe your family characteristics, roles, and rules, you may see some patterns across the three areas. This is very common and will give you an idea of how your patterns became part of you. Once you are clear about the patterns, you may choose to modify or make major changes to your response in the future. Looking for patterns helps you understand where you get stuck.

Did you discover a repeated pattern? _____

_____

_____

Then, you need to write out the pattern as you view it currently.

_____

_____

_____

Then write how you would like to change the pattern. _____

_____

_____

_____

_____

_____

It may be difficult to identify how you would like to do the pattern differently at this time. You may choose to come back to that part as you move further through the journaling process.

If you decide to do something differently, it is important to let everyone in the family know what you are changing. This is especially important with children. Otherwise, they will want you to return to old patterns that make you predictable. Children are very tuned in when parents are making pattern alterations. They respond well when they are included in understanding what you are doing and in the decision to do or be different.

Family characteristics, roles, and rules cover a broad cross-section of family functioning. Through identifying patterns and processes, you move your recovery forward to thriving in your life. You no longer carry the dysfunctional patterns of your childhood into your adult relationships and current family.

SECTION III

FEELINGS CENTERED JOURNALING

Feelings Centered Journaling

Experiencing feelings in-depth and delving deeper into them fully brings on an enhanced level of recovery. Keep in mind that feelings are not right or wrong, good or bad. They are your physical and emotional experience of life. As you move into work centered on feelings, you may find it difficult to acknowledge feelings and experience them.

DRAWING FACES TO REPRESENT FEELINGS

One technique I found helpful was to use face drawing to connect with the five basic feelings. Emoticons are a type of face drawings that often appear in e-mails. I strongly urge you to do your own drawings instead of looking at other drawings or emoticons. Take some basic feelings and create faces for each of them. You are able to connect visually before experiencing them physically. Draw 5 circles and put down the first thing that comes to mind for each feeling. *Draw faces for: Happy, Sad, Angry, Guilty, and Ashamed.*

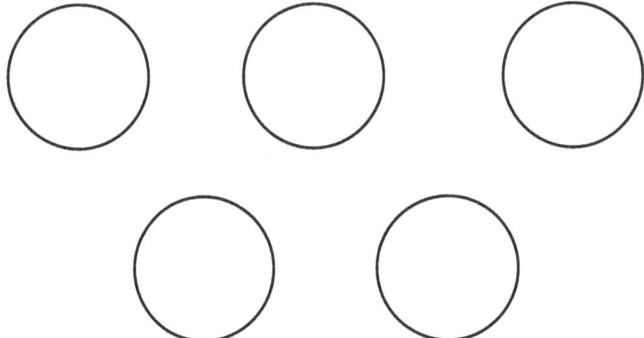

These often become confused with unclear messages from parents. *Get a clear picture of your understanding of the differences in these feelings from facial expressions, body language, and tone of voice.*

Guilty and ashamed look the same in this way: _____
_____
_____

Guilty and ashamed look different in this way: _____
_____
_____

Write about how these match or don't match for you _____
_____
_____

What do you need to transform to make feelings, facial expressions, body language, and tone of voice match? _____
_____
_____

How do you want to transform feelings to make facial expressions, body language, and tone of voice match? _____
_____
_____

DESCRIBING FEELINGS

The most effective method in describing a feeling is using your five senses and painting a word picture. I realized how cut off my body was from my brain. Thinking back to my five senses helped me connect my body and brain.

You may be wondering why this is such an important area for recovery. Feelings are the basis of healthy communication. When we are disconnected from our feeling self, we tend to express ourselves in dysfunctional ways.

For instance, we may use anger or hurt to lash out at someone we love very much instead of expressing our anger or hurt in a loving way. We may resort to passive/aggressive behaviors that hurt us and the people we love. We are unable to express verbally what is in our hearts. Therefore, we act out our feelings based on the patterns we learned in our families growing up.

> *Begin this Transformational Journaling technique by using your five senses to describe a feeling you have experienced in the last twenty-four hours. Describe the feeling using the prompts in each area of the descriptor table (Table 3). After describing an area, such as sight, tie the descriptor to a concrete object that helps you to visualize what you are describing in more detail.*

For example, if the feeling is jovial, ask yourself *"does your feeling have a shape, a color, a form? And that shape is like what? <u>Round.</u> And that color is like what? <u>Bright multi-colored.</u> And that form is like? <u>A big beach ball.</u>*

Texture description: Feels to the touch like <u>energy in motion</u> like what <u>an active squirming, child</u> Texture is <u>vibrating solid</u> like what <u>body jumping, quivering.</u>

Physical description: Where in body? <u>head to toe</u> Aware of body ache, tension, discomfort? <u>excited tension.</u>

Temperature description: Specific temperature Hot, warm, cold? <u>hot—85.</u>

Taste description: Tastes like? <u>yummy,</u> like what? <u>cold ice cream on a hot day.</u>

Sound description: Sounds? <u>marching band</u> like what? <u>playing happy music.</u>

Smell description: Smells? <u>sweet</u> like what? <u>cotton candy.</u>

Age: How old or young do you feel? <u>16.</u>"

My word picture is filled with brightness, happiness, and celebration that recall upbeat times in my life.

Proceed this way through each area until you understand and experience your feeling at a physical level using Describing Feelings (Table 3).

Table 3 Describing Feelings

SIGHT...............DOES YOUR FEELING HAVE A SHAPE? DOES YOUR FEELING HAVE A COLOR? DOES YOUR FEELING HAVE A FORM?

TEXTURE.............HOW DOES YOUR FEELING FEEL TO THE TOUCH? WHAT TEXTURE IS IT? ROUGH, SMOOTH, HOT, SOFT, HARD, WARM, COLD?

PHYSICAL............WHERE IN YOUR BODY DO YOU FEEL YOUR FEELING? STOMACH? HEAD? NECK? BACK? SHOULDERS? ARE YOU AWARE OF ANY PARTS OF YOUR BODY THAT ACHE, FEEL TENSE OR UNCOMFORTABLE?

TEMPERATURE.........DOES YOUR FEELING FEEL HOT, WARM OR COLD? A SPECIFIC TEMPERATURE?

TASTE...............DOES YOUR FEELING HAVE A TASTE? FOOD-SWEET, BITTER, SOUR, SMOOTH, ROUGH, SOFT, HARD, SLIPPERY?

SOUND...............WHAT SOUND DOES YOUR FEELING HAVE? MUSICAL INSTRUMENTS? NOISY, LOUD, SOFT, HARSH, SQUEEKY, KNOCKING, CRACKING, SINGING?

SMELL...............DOES YOUR FEELING HAVE A SMELL? FOOD-YUM, SOUR, GOOD, FRESH, STINKS, PERFUMY (FLOWERS), SWEET?

AGE................HOW OLD OR YOUNG DO YOU FEEL WHEN YOU EXPERIENCE THIS FEELING?

PAINT A WORD PICTURE TO HELP SOMEONE ELSE EXPERIENCE YOUR FEELING AS YOU EXPERIENCE IT.

Start out by identifying a feeling each day and writing your responses to the descriptors in your journal.

The feeling I am experiencing is _____

Sight description: Shape is _____
like what? _____ *Color is* _____
like what? _____ *Form is* _____
like what? _____

Texture description: Feels to the touch _____
like what? _____
Texture is _____ *like what?* _____

Physical description: Where in body? _____ *Aware of body ache, tension, discomfort* _____

Temperature description: Hot, warm, cold? Specific temperature _____
_____ *like what?* _____

Taste description: Tastes _____
like what? _____
Sound description: _____
like what? _____

Smell description: Smells _____
like what? _____

Age: How old or young you feel?

You painted a word picture that expresses your feeling to yourself and others. You made it real so you can connect with it. Help others to connect with you when you share life experiences on a feeling level.

You may find you are unable to describe your feeling in all the areas. Initially, this is fairly common and changes over time with practice. The next step toward building this emotional muscle is doing this exercise regularly. Take one feeling each day and use this technique until you are comfortable communicating your feelings

Once you feel comfortable with this step, find a close friend, therapist, sponsor, or another safe adult (wait to share with your intimate partner until you practice with others) to practice sharing feelings. You need to let this person know you are doing this. Give them the *Describing Feelings* information.

After this process becomes comfortable, then you are ready to share with your partner and other family members. (By this time, you are very clear that feelings are your experience and someone else's judgment is invalid.) Finally, I suggest you share your feelings with acquaintances and strangers.

This may seem odd since you are revealing yourself. Here is an example of how I use this with strangers. When I am talking to a customer service representative about a product problem, I might start the conversation by indicating I am very disappointed with the product and want to know my options regarding the product. This approach is very uncommon and usually gets their attention. I continue to focus the conversation in this tone and usually end up with what I want the outcome to be.

As you use this communication technique, especially with family members, the more effective your communications will become. You may notice children and life partners begin to communicate with you in the same manner. (See Appendix A for a list of feeling words. You may find you want to add words to the list.)

CARRIED FEELINGS

These are the feelings parents were not being responsible for within themselves when they were in their own shame. These feelings are the burdens weighing the recovering soul down because they override their own feelings. When a parent or other authority figure is experiencing anger but refuses to own their own anger and dumps it on their child, it comes out in the child as rage.

As an example, if a child is digging up the garden to see what makes the plants grow and mother finds him, her scolding may take the form of "you make me so angry, I'm going to spank you and send you to your room for the rest of the day". Now the child does not have the power to **make** the parent angry, ***this is the parent's feeling*** about having her garden dug up. By not owning the feeling, she gives it to the child who adds it on top of the hurt from being misunderstood about what he was doing. When he gets "caught" as an adult seemingly in similar circumstances all the stuffed anger for being misunderstood comes out in rage. He cannot express himself because his feelings come boiling to the surface and he reacts based on old messages instead of communicating what is going on in the present.

Some carried feelings include:

- anger is carried as rage
- pain(sadness) is carried as despair or hopelessness;
- fear is carried as terror;
- shame is carried as worthlessness;
- guilt is carried as shame;
- loneliness is carried as isolation or needlessness (Pia Mellody, 1986).

When you are able to experience your own feelings instead of carried feelings, you move forward in your life. Each of these pairs has an attached gift helping you overcome your former response pattern.

When you feel your own feelings, you experience them and the gifts they bring. The gift of experiencing your own anger is strength; pain is healing; fear is wisdom; shame is humility; guilt is your values; loneliness is connecting with others.

To release carried feelings, first write them in your journal, figure out what belongs to your parents, or significant adults from your childhood, and gently write out what feelings you are giving back. Explain how these Carried Feelings prevent you from moving forward in your recovery process.

> *My carried feeling of* _____
> *is what belongs to* _____
>
> *I give you back your feelings of* _____
> _____
>
> *Carrying your feelings of* _____ *prevents me from moving my life forward positively.*
>
> *I claim for myself my feelings of* _____
> _____
> _____

Pause after you complete this exercise to determine how you are feeling currently. Do you notice any change? What is the change? Continue this process with each carried feeling attached to each person who gave you their feelings.

GRIEF AND LOSS

Recovery involves grieving various types of losses in your life. You may grieve the loss of parental love, parental safety, or parental involvement in your life. Although your parents may still be living, you might find it emotionally and sometimes physically safer to remain detached from them. You may find it helpful to make this decision with a therapist who understands recovery.

Other areas where many people in recovery go through grieving are: loss of a relationship, loss of an addictive behavior pattern, or loss of a career. No matter what the loss, an important part of recovery is experiencing the grieving process.

The stages of grief defined by Elisabeth Kubler-Ross are: denial, anger, bargaining, depression and acceptance. What occurs in each of these stages is a process of letting go allowing for change to occur. This letting go is very painful and requires some conscious work. The outcome is a sense of freedom and ability to create a more peaceful and serene life.

The process works by a series of mood and behavior changes as you work through an event. Grieving may take as short as 30 seconds or more than a year. You may move from one stage to the next and back to a previous stage as you get in touch with more feelings.

To help you work through the grieving process, I devised five questions based on the five stages of grief. These questions are designed to help you assess where you are in your process and where you want to go to move through the grieving process. They are: What is the loss? What is the cause of the anger? How am I bargaining? What is causing my depressed feelings? How have I accepted the loss? You may find yourself coming back to these questions several times on the same issue as you work through the process.

One woman who used this process was finally able to let go of a very destructive relationship. This freed her to develop a healthy relationship with a very caring man. This was a positive situation eventually leading to remarriage and a healthy blended family.

There is no set order to work through grief. You may find yourself bouncing in and out of the different stages as you do your grief work. This is normal and there is no set time limit on how long it takes to grieve a loss. It is very important to be gentle with yourself while working through your grief. Once you reach acceptance, identify the steps you need to take to move on with your life.

Journal on the following five questions connected with the five stages of grief.

What is the loss? _____

_____

What is the cause of the anger? _____

_____

How am I bargaining? _____

_____

What is causing my depressed feelings? _____

_____

How have I accepted the loss? _____

_____

_____

> *What are the steps I need to take to get on with my life?*_____
>
> _____
>
> _____

After you work through a particular loss, you may feel your work is finished. However, be aware grief may reoccur on the anniversary of a loss. This is a common situation. Take a few minutes to journal about the anniversary event using the five grief questions. You will find you return to acceptance quickly.

Loss anniversaries tend to happen more often at five year intervals. They may reoccur when your child is at the same age you were when you experienced a loss. You may experience grief feelings when you approach major life events.

Connecting with you on a feeling level is an important process in recovery and transforming yourself. Use the processes of face drawings, describing feelings, releasing carried feelings, and grieving losses. They are all very important to recovering your soul, transforming, and recreating your life.

SECTION IV

THOUGHT CENTERED JOURNALING

Focusing on your thinking processes is an important area for recovering your soul. Many messages you received growing up continue to run your life at a subconscious level. You may find yourself on automatic pilot more than you can imagine. Your reactions to situations may seem to come out of nowhere. Actually, they are coming from messages received as a child. These messages affect your emotional and physical *boundaries.* Your *personal values, standards, and beliefs* are affected. They affect your *thinking in extremes.* Explore these areas and identify what thinking patterns are keeping you from recovering your soul.

BOUNDARY SETTING

Establishing Healthy Emotional and Physical Boundaries is an important area for transforming your life in recovery. Because recovering souls often experience boundary violations from abuse, neglect, or being burdened with carried feelings, they have difficulty setting and maintaining healthy boundaries. As you review your personal boundaries, consider in what settings you are functional and what settings you are dysfunctional and how that looks. By describing your experiences, you clearly see what you want to maintain and what you want to transform.

People seeking recovery often experienced boundary violations that leave one or more conditions present in their functioning. Boundary violations can leave a person totally vulnerable or totally invulnerable or somewhere in between. Being vulnerable means you can be taken advantage of or easily manipulated. A person who is totally vulnerable has no boundaries. They take everything personally. Often, they accept responsibility for others actions even when they are totally uninvolved. Their communication is based on what they think the other person wants to hear. They believe everything someone tells them about who they are.

A person who is totally invulnerable will have walls. *Walls* are solid barriers that prevent communication from coming in or going out. They operate strictly from their view of the world and refuse to consider any information that is outside their self-understanding.

A person with *damaged boundaries* may experience walls around some issues and some level of vulnerability around other issues. A person with damaged boundaries will have areas of vulnerability and areas of invulnerability.

A person with *functional boundaries* is able to allow healthy communication and to deflect unhealthy communication. They receive feedback and determine if it is accurate before deciding to act on it or not.

As you assess your boundaries, determine your response to communication based on the above conditions. An easy way to make this assessment is to connect with your feeling state when you receive either verbal or written communication. If your response is neutral, then you are probably operating with a functional boundary around that communication. If your response is highly emotional, then you may be operating from either no boundaries or damaged boundaries. If your response is numbness, then you are probably operating from walls.

> *Questions to ask in journaling around boundaries are: 1) what is my reaction, on an emotional level, to the communication I just received?*
>
> _____
>
> _____
>
> *2) How is that reaction like or unlike my normal response pattern?*
>
> _____
>
> _____
>
> *3) How do I want to respond to a similar communication in the future?*
>
> _____
>
> _____

When setting healthy boundaries, it is helpful to know in advance how you want to respond so you are no longer caught off guard. This means you either over-react or under-react to the communication. Your journal is a good way to plan out these responses. It is an effective reference point if you detect a certain pattern over time.

Identifying your *Personal values, standards, and beliefs* helps to establish healthy boundaries. Values, standards, and beliefs are integrated from daily involvement with family and primary authority figures in our lives. As adults, we often find ourselves responding to situations just as we experienced responses from our parents. You may have silently committed to behaving differently with your children only to find the same response occurring when similar circumstances arise. These responses may come from one or both parents, clergy, teachers, or other primary relationships in your life.

In order to consciously choose a different response, it is important to **identify the different situations** _____

_____

_____

Determine where you received *your values, standards, and beliefs related to that situation* _____

_____

_____

Determine if you want to keep your belief *as you learned it or* **how you want to transform your belief** *based on your current value system.* _____

_____

_____

Write out in detail **how you want to transform your value, belief, or standard** *so that you can respond without deep thinking when a situation presents itself.* _____
_____
_____
_____
_____
_____

For example, take the area of character values, standards and beliefs. Write out answers to the following questions.

What kind of person do you want to be? _____
_____
_____

What kind of attitudes about yourself do you want to have?
_____
_____
_____

What kind of attitudes about others do you want to have? _____
_____
_____

What kind of behavior characterizes you? _____
_____

> *What kind of different behaviors would you like to have?*
>
> _____
>
> _____
>
> _____

Other areas for evaluating your values, standards, and beliefs are:

- relationships with the opposite sex or same sex
- family
- recreation
- social
- spiritual
- educational
- career
- financial

Consider your expectations, your attitudes, how to spend your time, level of importance, money involvement, and your responsibilities in each area. Values, standards, and beliefs are tied closely with your goals and maintenance of a transformed lifestyle.

POLARIZED THINKING

Another area where boundary violations occur is in our thinking processes. People entering recovery often find they have rigid thinking patterns. They tend to be black and white, or either or thinking patterns. I like to think of them as opposite ends of a teeter-totter. When you choose your response from one end or the other, you are out-of-balance.

Where did you learn to operate from in a thinking mode? Your parents, primary authority figures, or other significant adults in your life while you were growing up, are where to look first. Did they send specific messages about how to think about certain events? Did they allow for balance or grey areas?

One couple I worked with found they each operated at the opposite end of the teeter-totter. They were constantly in conflict over trying to change the other person to their way of thinking. They were unable to come toward the balance point. This helped them decide what they wanted to change in their relationship.

Review the extremes and describe how each extreme operates in your life.
Extreme described _____

_____

_____

_____

Review the balance points and determine how you want to transform yourself to come into balance. Balance point described _____

_____

_____

_____

> *As you journal, be as descriptive as possible so you can easily identify when you are operating with polarized thinking. You may find it necessary to experience the opposite thinking process in order to find your healthy balance point.*

When you review Table 4, you may find other polarized thinking patterns that are not listed. Using the table as a model, construct both ends of the continuum and identify a healthy balance point for extremes you discover in your life.

Table 4 Polarized Thinking

EXTREME	BALANCE POINT	EXTREME
Passive Control	Self-control	Active control
Irresponsible	Self-responsible	Super-responsible
Needy	Asks for wants & needs	Needless
Vulnerable	Shares appropriately	Invulnerable
Super-caring	Emotionally intimate	Non-involvement
Aggressive	Assertive	Passive
Leader only	Team member	Follower only
Enmeshed	Interconnected	Disengaged
Minimizing	Reality based	Catastrophizing
Over-reactive	Responsive	Numb
Independent	Interdependent	Dependent
Low self-esteem	Self-esteemed	Arrogance/grandiose
No boundaries	Functional boundaries	Walls
Chaos	Imperfect/fallible	Perfectionistic
Powerful	Empowered	Powerless
Fearful	Self-control	Overly controlled
Invisible	Being seen	Highly visible
Shamed	Fallible	Shameless
Attention (constant)	Positive Recognition	Abandonment
Anger(Passive)	Assertive feelings	Anger(Aggressive)
Greed	Abundance	Scarcity
Win	Win-Win	Lose
Open	Flexible/Receptive	Closed
Love	Tolerance/Respect	Hate

Thought centered journaling is a vital area to address in recovery. You may react to messages and communication without considering what thought processes are behind your reactions. Then, as you consider the situation at a later time, you may find yourself wishing you said something differently or reacted in a different way. Being aware of your personal boundaries, helps you adjust your reaction to respond based on choice. Awareness of your polarized thinking allows you the opportunity to choose your verbal response instead of automatically reacting with the thinking patterns you learned in childhood.

SECTION V

MAINTAINING RECOVERY

Maintaining recovery involves daily action through *affirmations, creating a balanced lifestyle,* and *establishing realistic goals.* When focused on what you want to be, have, and do, you are moving forward to create your life. You are in charge and every choice you make moves you forward to living life on your terms.

AFFIRMATIONS

Affirmations are an important part of integrating the transformations you have chosen in your journaling process. Create affirmations at any point in your recovery process using the changes you have created in your journal responses. Develop brief, positive statements you can reinforce on a daily basis.

Prior to creating your affirmation cards, *divide a blank sheet of paper in half. In the left column write down all the messages you want to change or the negative messages you remember receiving as a child. On the right side, write positive statements for change that offset the negative messages received.* Positive change messages are put on yellow 3 x 5 cards.

Messages to change (Negatives)	Positive Statements (Affirmations)

Early in my recovery, I learned the power of the color yellow to draw the eye. Without going into detail, I strongly recommend you write all your affirmations on yellow cards or yellow paper. There are some simple rules about writing affirmations which contribute to their power.

- *First, affirmations are written in the present as if they have already happened.*
- *Second, affirmations are written in the first person using "I am" or I have" as the beginning of your statement.*
- *Third, affirmations are written in positive language.*

If you decide to record your affirmations to listen to them, then you would dictate them in the second person. They would start with "You are" or "You have". The brain automatically converts them to first person.

Another important point to remember when formulating your affirmations is to eliminate the word "not" in any affirmation. The sub-conscious mind rejects the word "not" and is unable to hear it. Any affirmations written with the word "not" have the opposite effect. This is extremely important or you will affirm messages you are trying to change. One way to write positive affirmations is to eliminate the word "not" from everything you say or write for a week. Think POSITIVES ONLY!! You will find some dramatic results and find ways to rephrase negative sentences into positive ones.

> *Affirmation (written positively, starting with)*
>
> I am_____
>
> _____
>
> _____
>
> _____
>
> I have_____
>
> _____
>
> _____
>
> _____

An example of misusing "not" happens in letter writing. Many times at the close of a letter this common phrase occurs. "Please don't hesitate to call if you have questions." This gives the opposite message which is please don't call. To rewrite this in the affirmative, I say, "Please feel free to call with any questions." Try it this week and see what happens.

Daily use of affirmations is recommended as you are trying to change many years of negative messages said to you many times. It takes approximately 100 positives to offset one negative message. Most of the messages you received were said more than once. Then, you continued to repeat them through self-talk. Therefore, it is important to offset your automatic negative self-talk with repeated positive messages.

For especially *tough areas* to change behavior or thinking patterns, *write out your affirmation 21 times, three times a day, for 21 days. Divide your paper lengthwise with two thirds on the left side and one third on the right side. As you write out your affirmation and say it aloud, note in the right-hand column what the voice in your head is saying.*

Affirmation   *Voice in my head*

Over time, you will see the negative messages tied to the affirmation begin to drop off. At the end of 21 days, if you feel the negative messages are still strong, repeat this for another 21 days.

CREATING A BALANCED LIFESTYLE

Moving your recovery process along requires maintenance of all you accomplished through your transformational journaling process. There are many options for *creating a balanced lifestyle. By examining each area of your life, and determining where you are in that area and projecting where you would like to be in that area in one year, five years, and so forth, you begin to develop a framework for a balanced life.* As a beginning, look at the following areas:

- career
- financial
- home
- family
- spiritual
- ethical
- mental
- educational
- social
- cultural
- physical
- health

Each of these areas needs balance for a person to function in healthy ways. You can assess your current levels in each area to find out if you are in balance by using the following continuum with 1 being the least desirable and 10 being the most desirable level.

$$\underline{1 \quad 2 \quad 3 \quad 4 \quad 5 \quad 6 \quad 7 \quad 8 \quad 9 \quad 10}$$
Least desirable   Most desirable

Once you determine which areas you want to develop and which areas need to be maintained at their present level, you are now ready to look at how to accomplish this. Many people in recovery have issues around asking for their wants or needs to be met. One way to determine your wants and needs is to make a list of them.

> *Take a clean sheet of paper and write on the top "Everything I've ever wanted to do, be, or have", let yourself dream.*
> _____
> _____
> _____
> _____
> _____
> _____
> _____

Remember, you are the only one to see this list so allow yourself the freedom to put down anything you ever dreamed of doing, wanting, or being.

> *Now take your dream list and decide which of the areas of life they fall into and put that next to the items.*
>
> Career_____
> Financial_____
> Home_____
> Family_____
> Spiritual_____
> Ethical_____
> Mental_____
> Educational_____
> Social_____
> Cultural_____
> Physical_____
> Health_____

In order to achieve your dreams, it is necessary to know how you will do it. Start by *writing out your goals*. I recommend using the SMART model.

SMART stands for:

*S*pecific_____

*M*easurable_____

*A*ttainable_____

*R*isky_____

*T*imely_____

Goal statements are written positively, as if they already happened. This alerts your subconscious mind of your intention and motivates you to action.

> **Write out one goal:**_____
> _____
>
> *S*pecific_____
> *M*easurable_____
> *A*ttainable_____
> *R*isky_____
> *T*imely_____

In order to maintain recovery, a consistent check-up is necessary. One way to do this is to review your goals and your plan for a balanced lifestyle every 6 months. You can do it more often if your life entails major changes more frequently.

SHARING WITH OTHERS

Now that you are journaling, what do you do with all your writing? Sharing with others is a process you can do on an informal or formal basis. You may have a friend who you consider a confidante. Practice sharing with your friend after explaining what you are doing. Ask your friend to listen without judgment. The purpose is for you to release the secrets keeping you stuck from transforming your life into the one you want to live.

If you are in a 12-step program, you may choose to share with your sponsor or someone who is supportive of your recovery process. Another option is to share with a therapist or member of the clergy.

As you move forward in your journaling process, remember to take your time and experience the journey. Share your joys and especially your sorrows with a close trusted friend, sponsor or therapist.

Maintaining recovery is a lifelong process. You may find times when your life seems to run smoothly and your journaling becomes infrequent. This is a natural progression. Enjoy the plateau and learn from your prior experience. This is a great time to keep a gratitude list.

As your life becomes filled with thriving and living the life you desire, you may find stressful times require you to review your feelings, thoughts, and behavior patterns. Now you have the techniques to use whenever it becomes necessary. Keep this book close at hand to move through those times quickly and efficiently.

Remember, I am with you along the journey. If you want to communicate with me, please go to my website: http://houseofpeacepubs.com

Please let me know how this journal helped in recovering your soul. Feel free to contact me at any time in the future. I want to know how you are progressing in transforming your soul and recreating your life.

APPENDIX A:

FEELING WORDS

ABANDONED	APPALLED	BORED	CLEVER
ABLE BODIED	APPRECIATED	BOWLED OVER	CLOSED
ABLE	APPRECIATIVE	BOXED	COMFORTABLE
ABSORBED	APPREHENSIVE	BOXED IN	COMFORTING
ACCEPTED	AROUSED	BRANDED	COMICAL
ACCEPTING	ARROGANT	BRAVE	COMMITTED
ACCOMPLISHED	ASSERTIVE	BREATHLESS	COMMUNICATE
ACTIVE	ASSURED	BREEZY	COMPASSIONATE
ADAMANT	ASTONISHED	BRILLIANT	COMPATIBLE
ADAPTABLE	ASTOUNDED	BRISTLING	COMPETENT
ADEQUATE	AT EASE	BROKEN HEARTED	COMPETITIVE
ADMIRED	ATTACKING	BROKEN DOWN	COMPLETE
ADORED	ATTENTIVE	BROODING	CONCERN
ADVENTUROUS	ATTRACTED TO	BROTHERLY	CONDEMNED
AFFECTIONATE	ATTRACTIVE	BRUTAL	CONFIDENT
AFRAID	AUTHORITATIVE	BUBBLY	CONFUSED
AGGRAVATED	AWE STRUCK	BULLYING	CONGENIAL
AGGRESSIVE	AWED	BUOYANT	CONNECTED
AGHAST	AWKWARD	BURNED	CONSCIENCE-STRICKEN
AGITATED	BAFFLED	BUSTLING	
AGONIZING	BASHFUL	BUSY	CONSCIENTIOUS
AGONY	BEATEN	CALLOUS	CONSIDERATE
AGREEABLE	BEAUTIFUL	CALM	CONSIDERED
AGREEING	BELLIGERENT	CAPABLE	CONSIDERING
ALARMED	BELOW PAR	CAREFREE	CONTEMPLATIVE
ALERT	BENEVOLENT	CARING	CONTENTED
ALIENATED	BENIGN	CAST ASIDE	CONTRARY
ALIVE	BENT	CAUTIOUS	CONTROLLED
ALL IN	BEREAVED	CERTAIN	CONTRITE
ALONE	BETRAYED	CHAGRINED	COOL
ALTRUISTIC	BEWILDERED	CHALLENGED	COOPERATIVE
AMAZED	BIGHEARTED	CHANGEABLE	COP-OUT
AMBITIOUS	BITING	CHARITABLE	CORDIAL
AMIABLE	BITTER	CHARMED	CORNERED
AMOROUS	BLAMED	CHARMING	COURAGEOUS
AMUSED	BLESSED	CHEAPENED	COWARDLY
ANALYZING	BLISSFUL	CHEATED	CRANKY
ANGRY	BLUE	CHEERFUL	CREATIVE
ANNOYED	BLUNT	CHERISHED	CRIPPLED
ANXIOUS	BOASTFUL	CHICKEN- HEARTED	CRITICAL
APATHETIC	BOILING	CHILDISH	CROSS
APOLOGETIC	BOLD	CLEAR	CRUEL

Appendix A

CRUSHED	DISCOURAGED	EMOTIONAL	FIGHTING
CULPABLE	DISGRACED	EMPATHIC	FINE
CURIOUS	DISGUSTED	EMPTY	FIRED UP
CUT OFF	DISHONORED	ENCHANTED	FIRM
CYNICAL	DISLIKE	ENCOURAGED	FIT
DARING	DISLIKED	ENERGETIC	FLATTERED
DAZED	DISMAL	ENGROSSED	FLIRTATIOUS
DEBASED	DISMAYED	ENJOYING	FLUSTERED
DECREASE IN	DISORGANIZED	ENRAGED	FOND
DEDICATED	DISOWNED	ENTHUSIASTIC	FOOLISH
DEFEATED	DISPLEASED	ENVIOUS	FORCEFUL
DEFIANT	DISREPUTABLE	EQUAL TO THE TASK	FORGETFUL
DEFLATED	DISTRACTED		FORGIVING
DEFT	DISTRUSTFUL	ESCAPE(DESIRE TO)	FORLORN
DEGRADED	DISTURBED	ESTRANGED	FORSAKEN
DEJECTED	DOGMATIC	EVADING EVASIVE	FORTUNATE
DELIGHTED	DOMINATED	EVIL	FRAGILE
DEMEANED	DOMINEERING	EXALTED	FRAIL
DEMOLISHED	DONE FOR	EXASPERATED	FRANTIC
DENIAL	DOOMED	EXCELLENT	FREE AND EASY
DENOUNCED	DOUBTFUL	EXCITED	FRENZIED
DEPENDABLE	DOUBTING	EXCLUDED	FRETFUL
DEPENDENT	DOWNCAST	EXCUSES	FRIENDLESS
DEPRESSED	DOWNHEARTED	EXHAUSTED	FRIENDLY
DEPRIVED	DRAINED	EXHILARATED	FRIGHTENED
DESERTED	DREADING	EXPLAINING	FRIGID
DESERVING	DREARY	EXPOSED	FRISKY
DESIROUS	DROOPING	EXUBERANT	FROLICSOME
DESOLATE	DROWSY	FAILING	FRUSTRATED
DESPERATE	DUBIOUS	FAILURE	FULFILLED
DESPISED	DULL	FAIR	FULL
DESPONDENT	DUMFOUNDED	FAITHFUL	FUMING
DESTROYED	DYNAMIC	FALLING APART	FUN LOVING
DESTRUCTIVE	EAGER TO PLEASE	FANTASTIC	FUNCTION
DETESTING	EAGER	FASCINATED	FUNNY
DEVOTED	EASYGOING	FATALISTIC	FURIOUS
DIFFIDENT	ECSTATIC	FATHERLY	GALLANT
DIGNIFIED	ECSTATIC	FATIGUED	GAY
DILIGENT	EDGY	FAVORED	GENERALIZE
DIMINISHED	EFFECTIVE	FEARFUL	GENEROUS
DISAGREE	EFFICIENT	FEARLESS	GENIAL
DISAPPOINTED	ELATED	FEEBLE	GENTLE
DISAPPROVED OF	ELECTRIFIED	FEMININE	GENUINE
DISCARDED	ELEVATED	FEROCIOUS	GIDDY
DISCONTENTED	EMBARRASSED	FIERCE	GIFTED

GIVING	HONORABLE	INEFFECTIVE	LAUGHED AT
GLAD	HONORED	INEFFICIENT	LAUGHING
GLARING	HOPEFUL	INEPT INFERIOR	LECHEROUS
GLOOMY	HOPELESS	INFLAMED	LEFT OUT
GLORIOUS	HORRIBLE	INFURIATED	LENIENT
GLUM	HORRIFIED	INHIBITED	LET DOWN
GOOD	HOSPITABLE	INQUIRING	LICENTIOUS
GOOD HUMORED	HOSTILE	INQUISITIVE	LIFELESS
GRACIOUS	HUMANE	INSANE	LIGHT-
GRAND	HUMBLED	INSECURE	HEARTED
GRATEFUL	HUMILIATED	INSENSITIVE	LION HEARTED
GRATIFIED	HUMOROUS	INSINCERE	LIVELY
GREAT	HUNGRY	INSPIRED	LOATHING
GREEDY	HURT	INSUFFICIENT	LONELY
GRIEF	HYPERACTIVE	INSULTED	LONESOME
GRIEF STRICKEN	HYPOCRITICAL	INTELLECTUALIZE	LONG SUFFERING
GRIEVED	HYSTERICAL	INTELLIGENT	LONGING
GRIPPED	IDOLIZING	INTENSE	LONGING FOR
GROOVY	IGNORED	INTERESTED IN	LOSER, LIKE A
GRUDGE BEARING	IMAGINATIVE	INTIMIDATED	LOST
GRUDGING	IMMOBILIZED	INTOLERANT	LOVEABLE
GUILTY	IMPATIENT	INVESTIGATING	LOVED
GULLIBLE	IMPERFECT	INVOLVED	LOVING
HAPPY GO LUCKY	IMPORTANT	IRKED	LOW
HAPPY	IMPOTENT	IRRITATED	LOYAL
HARDY	IMPRESSED WITH	ISOLATED	LUCKY
HARSH	IN A COLD SWEAT	JARRED	LUSTFUL
HATEABLE	IN THE DUMPS	JEALOUS	MAD
HATED	IN A BIND	JILTED	MAGNIFICENT
HATEFUL	IN CONTROL	JITTERY	MAJESTIC
HEALTHY	IN HIGH SPIRITS	JOKING	MANIPULATED
HEARTLESS	IN TROUBLE	JOLLY	MANIPULATIVE
HEARTY	IN DOUBT	JOLTED	MANLY
HEAVENLY	IN CONTROL	JOVIAL	MARTYR
HEAVY HEARTED	INADEQUATE	JOYOUS	MARVELOUS
HELPFUL	INCAPABLE	JUBILANT	MASOCHISTIC
HELPLESS	INCENSED	JUDGED	MEAN
HEROIC	INCOMPETENT	JUDGMENTAL	MELANCHOLIC
HESITANT HIGH	INCOMPLETE	JUMPY	MELANCHOLY
HINDERED	INCONSISTENT	JUSTIFYING	MELLOW
HOLLOW	INDEBTED TO	KEEN	MERCIFUL
HOMELESS	INDECISIVE	KEYED UP	MERRY
HOMESICK	INDIGNANT	KIND	MIGHT
HOMICIDAL	INDEPENDENT	LACKING	MINDFUL
HONEST	INDIFFERENT	LACONIC	MIRTHFUL

MISCHIEVOUS	OVERLOOKED	PUNY	RESENTMENT
MISTRUSTFUL	OVERPOWERED	PUSHY	RESOURCEFUL
MISUNDERSTOOD	OVERWHELMED	PUT DOWN	RESPECTFUL
MIXED UP	PAINED	PUZZLED	RESPONSIBLE
MOPING	PANICKY	QUAKING	RESPONSIVE
MORALIZING	PARALYZED	QUALIFIED	RESTLESS
MOURNFUL	PARANOID	QUARRELSOME	RESTRAINED
MUDDLED	PASSIONATE	QUEASY	REVENGEFUL
MYSTIFIED	PATIENT	QUEER	REVERENT
NAGGED	PEACEFUL	QUESTIONING	REVIVED
NASTY	PEPPY	QUICK WITTED	REVOLTED
NAUSEATED	PERPLEXED	QUICKENED	REWARDED
NEED	PERSECUTED	QUIET	RIDICULOUS
NEEDY	PERTURBED	QUIVERING	RIGHTEOUS
NEGLECTED	PESSIMISTIC	RAGE	ROASTED
NEIGHBORLY	PETRIFIED	RAPTURE	ROBUST
NERVOUS	PHONEY	RATIONALIZE	ROUGH
NICE	PITY FOR OTHERS	RATTLED	RUDE
NIGGARDLY	PLACATING	RAVING	RUFFLED
NO GOOD	PLAYED-OUT	REASONING	RUINED
NONCHALANT	PLEASANT	READY TO	RUN DOWN
NUMB	PLEASED	EXPLODE	RUNNING AWAY
NUTTY	PLEASURE	REBELLIOUS	SAD
OBLIGING	POISED	REBUFFED	SADISTIC
OBNOXIOUS	POLITE	REBUKED	SAFE
OBSESSED	POMPOUS	RED FACED	SARCASM
OBSOLETE	PONDERING	REFLECTING	SARCASTIC
OBSTINATE	POSSESSIVE	REFRESHED	SATED
OCCUPIED	POTENT	REGRETFUL	SATIATED
OFFENDED	POUTFUL	REJECTED	SATISFIED
OLD	POWERFUL	REJECTION	SAVAGE
ON EDGE	POWERLESS	REJOICING	SCOFFED AT
OPEN	PRAISEFUL	RELAXED	SCORNED
OPPOSED	PREJUDICED	RELIABLE	SCREWED UP
OPTIMISTIC	PREOCCUPIED	RELIEF	SEARCHING
ORIGINAL	PRESSURED	RELIEVED	SECLUDED
OSTRACIZED	PRIM	RELIGIOUS	SECURE
OSTRACIZED	PRISSY	REMORSE	SEDUCTIVE
OUT OF CONTACT	PROJECTING	REMORSEFUL	SELF-COMPLACENT
OUT OF CONTROL	PROSPEROUS	RENEWED	SELF-CONFIDENT
OUT OF SORTS	PROTECTIVE	REPELLED	SELF-CONSCIOUS
OUTCAST	PROUD	REPRIMANDED	SELF-PITY
OUTRAGED	PROVOKED	REPULSED	SENSITIVE
OVER	PUNISHED	REPULSIVE	SERENE
OVERJOYED	PUNISHING	RESENTFUL	SETTLED

SELF-RELIANT	SPIRITED	SWITCHING	UNINVITED
SEXUALLY ABNORMAL	SPITEFUL	SYMPATHETIC	UNKIND
	SPLENDID	TAKEN ABACK	UNPOPULAR
SEXUALLY AROUSED	SPONTANEOUS	TANTALIZED	UNQUALIFIED
	SPORTIVE	TEARFUL	UNRESPONSIVE
SHAKEN	SPRIGHTLY	TENDER	UNRESTRAINED
SHAKY	SPRY	TENTATIVE	UNSELFISH
SHALLOW	SPURRED ON	TERRIBLE	UNSTABLE
SHAME	SQUELCHED	TERRIFIC	UNWELCOME
SHAMED	STABLE	TERRIFIED	UNWORTHY
SHARP	STAGGERED	THOUGHTFUL	USELESS
SHATTERED	STARTLED	THREATENED	VEHEMENT
SHEEPISH	STEAMED	THREATENING	VICIOUS
SHOCKED	STERN	THRILLED	VICTORIOUS
SHREWD	STIFLED	THWARTED	VIGOROUS
SHUNNED	STIMULATED	TICKLED	VINDICTIVE
SHY	STINGY	TIMID	VIOLENT
SICKENED	STORMY	TIRED	VITAL
SILENCE	STOUT-HEARTED	TOGETHER	VIVACIOUS
SILLY	STRAIGHT-FORWARD	TOLERANT	VULNERABLE
SINCERE		TORN	WALKED ON
SINFUL	STRAINED	TOUCHY	WANT
SKEPTICAL	STRANDED	TOUGH	WARM HEARTED
SKILLFUL	STRANGLED	TRAPPED	WARY
SLAMMED	STRONG	TREMBLING	WASHED OUT
SLIGHTED	STRUCK	TREMENDOUS	WEARY
SLUGGISH	STRUNG OUT	TRICKED	WEEPY
SMALL	STUFFED	TRIUMPHANT	WEIGHING
SMART	STUNNED	TROUBLED	WELL-SUITED
SMILING	STUPEFIED	TRUSTFUL WEAK	WELL OFF
SNEAKY	STUPID	TURNED ON	WHIPPED
SNEERING	STURDY	TWO-FACED	WHOLESOME
SNUBBED	SUCCESSFUL	UGLY	WICKED
SOCIABLE	SUFFOCATED	UNABLE TO	WISE
SOFT HEARTED	SUICIDAL	UNAMBITIOUS	WITHDRAWING
SOFT	SUITED	UNAPPRECIATED	WITHDRAWN
SOLEMN	SUNNY	UNASSUMING	WOEFUL
SOOTHED	SUNSHINY	UNCERTAIN	WONDERFUL
SORROWFUL	SUPERB	UNDERSTANDING	WORN OUT
SORRY	SUPERIOR	UNEASY	WORRIED
SORRY FOR	SUPPORTED	UNGAINLY	WORTHLESS
STUBBORN	SURE	UNGIFTED	WRECKED
SPARKLING	SUSPICIOUS	UNHAPPY	WRONG
SPEECHLESS	SWEET	UNIMPORTANT	YELLOW
SPINELESS	SWITCH	UNINHIBITED	ZANY

Journaling Pages

Journaling Pages

Journaling Pages

Journaling Pages

/ Journaling Pages

Journaling Pages

Journaling Pages

Journaling Pages

Journaling Pages

Journaling Pages

Journaling Pages

www.ingramcontent.com/pod-product-compliance
Lightning Source LLC
Chambersburg PA
CBHW032001080426
42735CB00007B/467